Guadalupe
body and soul

Marie-Pierre Colle

THE VENDOME PRESS

contents

introduction

"Guadalupe: Body and Soul" was born when I visited a nursery in Tepoztlán, not far from Mexico City. A young man in his twenties, who was selling cacti and pansies, caught my attention thanks to the large quantity of tattoos on his body. I suspected that he also had one of the Virgin of Guadalupe. He pulled up his T-shirt to show me his torso, and there it was stretching from his collarbone to his narrow waist. "Guadalupe is in my body and my soul," said the young gardener Juan Diego, named after the saint before whom the Virgin made her first appearance. This Virgin is also found on the back of many a Mexican prisoner who wants to avoid getting stabbed in a brawl with fellow inmates, and also on the dusty backs of illegal immigrants who cross the U.S. border, risking their lives to secure a better future. Guadalupe accompanies them northward, marked on their bodies like a shield that protects them from threats. Nobody attacks the Virgin as nobody would offend her image.

Summoning the Virgin can perform miracles. Among the many stories Mexicans have heard about kidnappings in Mexico City in recent years, one story moved me in particular. After weeks of negotiations between the family of an eight-year old and his captor, the boy's desperate young mother shouted into the telephone, "In the name of the Virgin of Guadalupe, return my son!" The kidnapper asked her "Are you a Guadalupana, señora?" That afternoon, the child was on his way back to his parents. This is one of the numerous occasions when Guadalupan solidarity can protect us.

The original image of the Virgin of Guadalupe and the flag of the Basilica of Guadalupe: two important Mexican icons.

The Virgin of Guadalupe defines Mexico. She is the flag, representing Mexicans' aspirations; she is the country's most important icon, the essence that binds it together. She accompanied Zapata during the Mexican Revolution just as she accompanies her many believers today in their everyday struggles. Guadalupe has become a symbol of Mexican national identity. She is larger than life, and is found in churches and most homes; her image is in offices, restaurants, markets, nightclubs, parking lots, and hospitals; she is in purses, on street corners and construction sites, and taxi drivers carry her in their wallets for protection. She can be seen at La Quebrada in Acapulco, where divers kneel down in front of her before plunging 150 feet into the sea, and near those cliffs children go to see her through the glass bottom boats, where there is an effigy of her underwater between the Caleta and Roqueta beaches. She is found on the T-shirts of the Monarch soccer team from Morelia in Michoacán, as well as on the T-shirt of the rock star Alex Lora.

The image of this patroness of printers can be found backstage in the National Auditorium in Mexico City, her image eight feet high, and there isn't an actor, dancer, or singer who doesn't entrust himself to her before going onstage. To commemorate the fiftieth anniversary of Mexico City's enormous bullring, a highly emotional ceremony was conducted in the center of the ring just before a "corrida." The "torero" Enrique Ponce, his elegant cape embroidered with the Virgin's image, walked around the periphery as his "cuadrilla" sang "Las Mañanitas," the local version of "Happy Birthday."

Guadalupe has ruled variously as La Virgencita, La Madrecita, and La Morenita ever since she appeared to Juan Diego in 1531. As every Mexican knows, the Virgin commanded Juan Diego, a simple Indian laborer, to build a church in her honor on the hill of Tepeyac, north of Mexico City. The Virgin miraculously imprinted her image on Juan Diego's "tilma," a cloth made from maguey fiber, which today is venerated in her famous Basilica of Guadalupe. The Virgin showered fragrant roses upon the wintery hillside, and convinced the Spanish bishop Don Fray Juan de Zumárraga of her identity; millions of pilgrims have prayed to her ever since. Today, more than ever, Guadalupe is Mexico's spiritual gift to the world: she is increasingly adored in the United States, South America, China, India, and Europe. She was named "Queen of Mexico, Empress of the Americas" in 1895 by the visionary Pope Léon XIII.

The myth of the Virgin was merged with the story of Tonantzin, the Pre-Colombian fertility goddess, a common practice used to convert indigenous peoples conflating pagan and Catholic deities and beliefs. The Virgin, who is also known as Tonantzin-Guadalupe, then assumed all the qualities associated with the pre-conquest Earth Mother, though believers prayed to her for any variety of reasons, not just prayers related to fertility or the fecundity of the land. Numerous are her blessings and miracles. "People don't always talk about them," a vegetable seller once told me in a marketplace, "but my godmother prays to Tonantzin-Guadalupe when she wants a good job, or simply to be treated well." Some people have revolving lamps in the form of the Virgin, and she rotates while blessing every nook and cranny of a room.

Twenty million people visit the Basilica of Guadalupe northeast of Mexico City every year, and particularly on December 12, her saint's Day. They come in processions from all over Latin America, walking or crawling on bleeding knees, by bus, bicycle, and on subway to join in this celebration. Prayers engender faith, and faith heals illness of the body, mind, and soul. Devotion to the Virgin, patron saint of the underprivileged, gives hope for a better life. At midnight, the basilica rocks and rolls when famous singers such as María Victoria, Lucero, Guadalupe Pineda, and Ramón Vargas sing "Las Mañanitas" to the sound of a mariachi.

The true miracle of the Virgin of Guadalupe is her overwhelming presence in the hearts of the Mexican people, millions of whom have tolerated the intolerable only because of their faith and devotion. She is Holy Mother to all Latinos and Chicanos—abroad her image covers entire walls side by side with that of Michael Jackson, Óscar Chávez, and other hugely popular artists. And after the events of September 11, 2001, she could be found in the ruins of the Twin Towers. Led by the renowned sprinter Ana Gabriela Guevara, family members of illegal U.S. immigrants jogged from the Basilica of Guadalupe all the way to New York, where they sought the legalization of 4,500,000 undocumented Mexicans. The runners transported the images of the Virgin and San Juan Diego across the border: symbolically, like the immigrants whose rights they were championing, they had no papers! The 3,127 mile journey concluded in the front of St. Patrick's Cathedral on December 12, 2002.

Guadalupe's influence on every aspect of Latin American culture is undeniable: her image graces fine and folk art alike. And reverence for her extends across the world: Pope John Paul II has a profound respect for the Virgin of Guadalupe, and he came to canonize San Juan Diego, as well as the Queen and Empress of Mexico in July 2002. He has said on various occasions that "Mexico needs its indigenous people just as the indigenous people need Mexico." With her image stamped in our hearts, bodies, and thoughts, Mexicans carry out Guadalupe's will as expressed in the "Nican Mopohua," the Aztec tale of the apparitions of Tepeyac, written by Antonio Valeriano in 1544, and included in this book in Spanish and English. In the words of the Virgin "I very much desire that they build my sacred little house here, where I may express and make self-evident all of my love, compassion, help and protection. Because in truth, I am your merciful mother, to you and to the inhabitants of this land and to all who love me, those who seek me; those who trust me."

In this book, we celebrate Tonantzin-Guadalupe, the great companion of Latinos throughout the year, without regard for who they are or where they live.

Marie-Pierre Colle

A fisherman in Zihuatanejo, Guerrero, has the image of La Morenita (the little dark-skinned Virgin) tattooed on his back as a pledge, in payment for "a little favor." Prisoners in jail also have her image tattooed on their backs so no one will stab them.

Marcos Bermejo Bravo

VIRGEN   MARIA DE GUADALUPE
TE PIDO   CON TODAS LAS
GANAS   DE MI CORAZON
QUE   SANES
MI   MANO, LO
MAS   PRONTO QUE
SI   PUEDA,
AYUDA   TANTO EN
MIS   ESTUDIOS
COMO   EN MI SALUD
Y   TAMBIEN
TE   ENCOMIENDO
Y   TODA MI
FAMILIA   Y MIS
SERES   QUERIDOS.
PROTEGE MI   PADRE Y MADRE
QUE ES EL REGALO MAS LINDO QUE ME
MI DIOS.

passion for the virgin

Here it is told, put in order
how a short time ago, in a monumental way,
the perfect maiden appeared,
Santa María, Mother of God,
our Noble Lady,
up in Tepeyac, summit of the mountain,
who is said to be Guadalupe.
First a little man appeared
by the name of Juan Diego.
Then Her precious image appeared
before the newly elected bishop
Don Fray Juan de Zumárraga,
and all of the marvels
performed by him [are also told].

And ten years after
the water, the mountains,
Mexico City were conquered,
the arrow, the shield reposed,
they laid in peace throughout
various towns.
Not only did they sprout then,
but the belief, the knowledge
of the bearer of life, of the true God,
grow ripe now; they unfold.
Then, in the year 1531,
some December days having elapsed, it happened.
There was a little man, a poor man,
his name was Juan Diego.
It is said that he lived in Cuauhtitlán.
And regarding the things of God,
they all belonged to Tlatelolco.

Aquí se relata, se pone en orden,
cómo, hace poco, de manera portentosa,
se mostró la perfecta doncella,
Santa María, madrecita de Dios,
nuestra noble señora,
allá en Tepeyac, Nariz del monte,
que se dice Guadalupe.
Primero se mostró a un hombrecillo,
de nombre Juan Diego.
Luego apareció su imagen preciosa
ante el recién electo obispo
don fray Juan de Zumárraga,
y [también se relatan] todas las maravillas
que ha hecho.

Y a diez años
de que fue conquistada el agua, el monte,
la ciudad de México,
ya reposó la flecha, el escudo,
por todas partes estaban en paz
en los varios pueblos.
No ya sólo brotó,
ya verdea, abre su corola
la creencia, el conocimiento
del Dador de la vida, verdadero Dios.
Entonces, en el año 1531,
pasados algunos días
del mes de diciembre, sucedió.
Había un hombrecillo, un pobrecillo,
su nombre era Juan Diego.
Se dice que tenía su casa en Cuauhtitlán.
Y en cuanto a las cosas divinas,
aún todo pertenecía a Tlatelolco.

Mother and her believer: the spirit of Guadalupe is expressed in a letter to the Virgin written on
a simple piece of notebook paper with her brightly colored image drawn in marker.

And it was saturday,	Y era sábado,
still very early morning,	todavía muy de mañana,
he was on his way to pursue divine worship	venía en seguimiento de las cosas divinas
and to carry out his errands.	y de lo que estaba mandado.
As he approached the little hill,	Y vino a acercarse al cerrito,
the one known as Tepeyac,	donde se llama Tepeyac,
dawn glistened upon the earth.	ya relucía el alba en la tierra.
He heard singing on the little hill,	Allí escuchó: cantaban sobre el cerrito,
like the song of many precious birds;	era como el canto de variadas aves preciosas.
when their voices ceased,	Al interrumpir sus voces,
it was as if the hill was answering them;	como que el cerro les respondía.
extremely soft and delightful,	Muy suaves, placenteros,
their songs exceeded the songs of the coyoltototl,	sus cantos aventajaban a los del pájaro cascabel,
the tzinizcan and of other precious birds.	del tzinitzcan y otras aves preciosas que cantan.
Juan Diego stopped	Se detuvo Juan Diego,
and said to himself:	se dijo:
Am I indeed worthy of what I hear?	¿Es acaso merecimiento mío
Perhaps I am merely dreaming?	lo que escucho?
Am I awakening from a dream?	¿Tal vez estoy sólo soñando?
Where am I?	¿Acaso sólo me levanto del sueño?
Where do I find myself?	¿Dónde estoy?
Is it possible that I am in the place	¿Dónde me veo?
our ancient ancestors, our grandparents, told us about,	¿Tal vez allá,
in the land of flowers,	donde dejaron dicho los ancianos,
in the land of corn, of our flesh,	nuestros antepasados, nuestros abuelos,
possibly in the land of heaven?	en la Tierra florida, Xochitlalpan,
	en la Tierra de nuestro sustento, Tonacatlalpan,
	tal vez allá en la Tierra celeste, Ilhuicatlalpan?

ABOVE, LEFT: Cyclists on a pilgrimage reach the old Basilica of Guadalupe. The sacred image protects their bicycles from getting stolen.

ABOVE, RIGHT: Near "the fountain" at the Universidad Iberoamericana in Mexico City, the Virgin is drawn with White-Out on a tree trunk, an important display of students' passion for the Virgin.

OPPOSITE: When the December 12th celebrations draw near, the sidewalks turn into makeshift beds, and the blessed image watches over the faithful.

He was looking over there,
toward the summit of the hill,
where the sun breaks,
from where the lovely celestial chant came;
and then the singing ceased
and there was silence.
He then heard a voice calling
from atop the peak
that said to him:
"Little Juan, Little Juan Diego."
Then he ventured
and went to where he was called.

Nothing frightened him,
Nor was he upset by this,
rather to the contrary: he was overjoyed;
he rejoiced.
Then he climbed the hill,
to see from where he was being called.
And when he reached the summit,
he saw a Noble Lady
standing before him.

She called him to Her side.
And when he arrived at Her presence,
she surpassed wonderful perfection
and she astonished him.
Her clothing glimmered
like the sun.
The rocks and stones
on which she stood
burst with brilliance
like precious jade trinkets that shone
and the earth glittered
like the rainbow.

Hacia allá estaba mirando,
hacia lo alto del cerrito,
hacia donde sale el sol,
hacia allá, de donde venía
el precioso canto celeste.
Cesó el canto,
dejó de escucharse.
Ya entonces oyó,
era llamado
de arriba del cerrito.
Le decían: Juanito, Juan Dieguito.
Luego ya se atrevió,
así irá a allá,
donde era llamado.

Nada inquietó su corazón,
ni con esto se alteró,
sino que mucho se alegró,
se regocijó.
Fue a subir al cerrito,
allá va a ver donde lo llamaban.
Y cuando llegó
a la cumbre del cerrito,
contempló a una noble señora
que allí estaba de pie.

Ella lo llamó,
para que fuera a su lado.
Y cuando llegó a su presencia,
mucho le maravilló
cómo sobrepasaba
toda admirable perfección.
Su vestido,
como el sol resplandecía,
así brillaba.
Y las piedras y rocas
sobre las que estaba
flechaban su resplandor
como de jades preciosos,
cual joyeles relucían.
Como resplandores de arco iris
reverberaba la tierra.

OPPOSITE AND ABOVE: A truck and a tricycle decorated with paper streamers, balloons, and flowers for the visit to the Villa, the area in which the Basilica of Guadalupe is located.
OVERLEAF: Each vehicle is like a float that joins the perpetual religious parade. Here, in the folds of Pico de Orizaba, Mexico's highest mountain, a team of pilgrims returns home.

MENSAJES A LA VIRGEN

The mesquite trees, prickly pear,	Y los mezquites, los nopales
and the other varied weeds	y las demás variadas yerbitas
that grow there	que allí se dan,
looked like Quetzal feathers,	se veían como plumajes de quetzal,
their foliage like turquoise,	como turquesas aparecía su follaje,
and their stems, their thorns, their little splinters	y su tronco, sus espinas, sus espinitas,
shimmered like gold.	relucían como el oro.

TOP, LEFT AND TOP, RIGHT: At dawn, pilgrims entering the basilica carry the holy images on their backs, bedecked with colored garlands.
ABOVE: The messages to the Virgin in this little wooden box in the chapel of Universidad Iberoamericana are requests for forgiveness for sins committed and expressions of sincere repentance.
OPPOSITE: The shawl encloses Guadalupan passion, which is demonstrated in prayer, silent supplication, and unseen weeping.
OVERLEAF: The Basilica of Guadalupe, designed by architect Pedro Ramírez Vázquez, holds 10,000 pilgrims. Mexicans go to the Villa to feel better, to give thanks for favors bestowed, to find inner peace, and to strengthen themselves spiritually.

24

He bowed before Her	Delante de ella se inclinó,
and heard	escuchó
Her sweet revered breath,	su reverenciado aliento, su reverenciada palabra,
Her very noble and revered word,	en extremo afable,
as if it attracted him	muy noble,
and showed him love.	como que lo atraía,
She said to him:	le mostraba amor.
"Listen my youngest son,	Le dijo ella:
little Juan, where are you going?"	Escucha, hijo mío, el más pequeño,
	Juanito, ¿a dónde vas?

ABOVE: An emotional mass with bullfighters and their "cuadrillas" in the ring of Mexico's monumental Plaza de Toros, in celebration of the plaza's fiftieth anniversary in 1996. The Virgin of Guadalupe and the Virgin of Macarena, Virgin of the bullfighters, lead the procession together.
OPPOSITE: The cape of bullfighter Enrique Ponce is embroidered with the image of the Virgin of Guadalupe, and adorns the altar used to celebrate the bullfighter's mass.

He replied:
"My Lady, Noble Lady,
Little Girl,
I will go to your sacred little house
in Tlatelolco,
I will follow the things of God,
that are taught to us by the ones
who are the images of God:
our priests."

She spoke to him in this way,
showing Her lovely being,
she said:
"Know that your heart is like this,
my little one,
the truth is that I am me,
the Ever Virgin Holy Mary,
Mother of the True God,
Giver of life, Ipalnemohuani,
Creator of all life, Teyocoyani,
Two-lord, God of all existence,
Tloque Nahauque
Lord of heaven and earth,
Ilhuicahua and Tlalticpaque.
I very much desire
that they build my sacred little house here
where I may express
and make self-evident

Y él le respondió:
Señora mía, noble señora,
mi muchachita,
me acercaré allá, a tu reverenciada casa
en México Tlatelolco,
voy a seguir las cosas divinas,
las que nos entregan,
nos enseñan
los que son imagen del Señor,
el Señor Nuestro, nuestros sacerdotes.

En seguida así le habla ella,
le muestra su preciosa voluntad,
le dice:
sábelo,
que esté así tu corazón,
hijo mío, el más pequeño,
en verdad soy yo
la en todo siempre doncella,
Santa María,
su madrecita de él, Dios verdadero,
Dador de la vida, Ipalnemohuani,
Inventor de la gente, Teyocoyani,
Dueño del cerca y del junto, Tloque Nahuaque,
Dueño de los cielos, Ilhuicahua,
Dueño de la superficie terrestre, Tlalticpaque.
Mucho quiero yo,
mucho así lo deseo
que aquí me levanten
mi casita divina,
donde mostraré,
haré patente,

TOP: An elderly woman wearing an embroidered blouse and traditional shawl prays to the Virgin, full of affection and trust.
ABOVE: Tarahumara Indians in their regional dress accompany the sacred images and take them to be blessed.
OPPOSITE: A young pilgrim protects herself from the sun with an embroidered satin banner with the Virgin's image surrounded by roses.

all of my love,
compassion,
help and protection.
Because in truth,
I am your merciful mother,
to you and to the inhabitants
of this land
and to all who love me,
those who seek me;
those who trust me.

entregaré a las gentes
todo mi amor,
mi mirada compasiva,
mi ayuda, mi protección.
Porque, en verdad, yo soy
vuestra madrecita compasiva,
tuya y de todos los hombres
que vivís juntos en esta tierra
y también de todas las demás gentes,
las que me amen,
los que me llamen, me busquen,
confíen en mí.

I will listen to their call
and their sorrow,
and I will rectify
and remedy their needs,
miseries, and their sorrows.
And to accomplish
what I represent,
go to the palace of the bishop of Mexico.

Allí en verdad oiré
su llanto, su pesar,
así yo enderezaré,
remediaré todas sus varias necesidades,
sus miserias, sus pesares.
Y para que sea realidad lo que pienso,
lo que es mi mirada compasiva,
ve allá al palacio
del obispo de México.

On December 12th in the Villa of Guadalupe, banners from many parts of Mexico represent different barrios, suburbs, and towns. Indigenous groups carry them with pride and dignity.

And tell him that I send you	Y le dirás cómo te envío
to reveal	para que le muestres
how much I want him to build me	cómo mucho deseo
a sacred house here, on the plain.	que aquí se me haga una casa,
You may tell him	se me levante mi casa divina en el llano.
all you have seen	Bien le contarás
and admired,	todo cuanto viste,
all that you have heard.	lo que te ha admirado,
	y lo que oíste.
Know that I will be most grateful	Y que así esté tu corazón,
and truth be known,	porque bien lo agradeceré,
I will reward you in abundance;	lo compensaré,
I will make you worthy	en verdad así te daré en abundancia,
of your recompense.	te enalteceré.

ABOVE, LEFT: The Virgin is wearing a red velvet cape trimmed in white imitation fur and a tiara, like a queen of the carnival.

ABOVE, RIGHT: For those who prefer a more traditional keepsake, one can take a photograph at the Virgin's side with a sign reading: "Am I not here, I, who am your mother?"

OPPOSITE: A young girl mounts a white hobby horse for a commemorative picture of her visit to the Basilica of Guadalupe.

And you will be aptly worthy
thus I will compensate you
for your effort and fatigue
in that you will obtain
what I have entrusted in you.
You have heard, my youngest son,
my breath and my word;
Go now with all your effort."

Then he bowed before Her
and said:
"My Lady, my Noble Lady,
I will faithfully comply
with Your revered breath and word;
thus I leave You now,
I, Your humble servant."

Then he descended
to comply with the errand,
and went to find the road
leading directly to Mexico City.
When he entered the city
he went directly to the bishop's palace,
the governing priest
who had just recently arrived,
Don Fray Juan de Zumárraga,
priest of San Francisco.

He tried to approach
and then see him;
he pleaded with the servants
to announce his arrival.
After a long wait
he was called
and advised that the bishop would see him.
So he entered,
and bowed,
and on bended knee before the prelate
he delivered
the revered message
from the Lady from heaven.
He also recited
all that had astonished him,
all that he saw and heard.

Y mucho allí merecerás,
así yo te recompensaré
por tu fatiga, tu trabajo,
con que irás a cumplir
a lo que yo te envío.
Ya escuchaste, hijo mío el más pequeño,
mi aliento, mi palabra.
Ve ya,
hazlo con todo tu esfuerzo.

Luego él ante ella se postró,
le dijo:
señora mía, noble señora,
en verdad ya voy, cumpliré
tu reverenciado aliento, tu reverenciada palabra.
Así pues ahora te dejo,
yo tu pobre servidor.

Luego vino a bajar
para ir a cumplir su encargo,
vino a encontrar la calzada
que va derecho a México.
Cuando llegó al interior de la ciudad,
luego se fue derecho al palacio del obispo,
el cual hacía poco había llegado,
el gobernante de los sacerdotes,
su nombre era don fray Juan de Zumárraga,
sacerdote de San Francisco.

Y fue a acercarse,
luego trata de verlo,
suplica a los que le sirven,
a sus criados,
que vayan a decirle.
Ya un poco se hizo larga la espera.
Vienen a llamarlo,
ya lo dispuso el que gobierna, obispo,
así entrará.
Y ya entró,
en seguida ante él se pone de rodillas,
se inclina.
Luego ya le hace manifiesto,
le comunica
su reverenciado aliento, su reverenciada palabra
de la noble señora del cielo,
lo que es su mensaje.
También le refiere
todo lo que le había maravillado,
lo que vio, lo que escuchó.

TOP, LEFT: The flower vendors of Jamaica Market in Mexico City are famous for their floral arrangements; a crown of chrysanthemums on a bed of pine branches frames La Morenita (the little dark-skinned Virgin) of Tepeyac.

TOP, RIGHT: In the Villa of Guadalupe, a child dressed in traditional indigenous attire celebrates the Feast of Corpus Christi, a Mexican tradition. Her hair is braided with ribbons and covered with a "rebozo" (a Mexican shawl); paper necklaces and flowers enhance her colorful dress.

ABOVE, LEFT: The Virgin of Guadalupe, surrounded by roses, carries an enormous sunflower in her hands.

ABOVE, RIGHT: A Yucatec woman poses for her keepsake photo to remember her visit to the Villa. Embroidered flowers adorn her "huipil" (traditional blouse), just as silk flowers adorn the Virgin.

After having heard his whole story
and message,
it seemed unbelievable.
The bishop said to him:
"You will return, my son,
and I will listen to you more thoughtfully
and will consider it from the beginning
and contemplate
what will and desire
could have brought you here."

Pero el obispo cuando oyó todo su relato,
su mensaje,
como que no le pareció muy verdadero.
Le respondió el obispo, le dijo:
Hijo mío, otra vez vendrás,
más despacio te escucharé,
así desde el comienzo veré,
pensaré qué te ha traído,
lo que es tu voluntad,
lo que es tu deseo.

ABOVE, LEFT: The "boss" is always at the forefront of Mexican fiestas and traditions. Here she appears on the front of a child's straw hat, whose face is painted with a moustache and beard.

TOP, RIGHT: Traditional wear for fiestas donned by the men of Zacapoaxtla, in the state of Puebla, is lovingly embroidered by a mother or wife with the Virgin's image, and also includes strings of beads and silky bows.

ABOVE, RIGHT: Young or old, criollo or mestizo, a general, a worker or college graduate, the Mexican seems to me like the image in which he encloses and preserves himself: masking the face and masking his smile," writes Octavio Paz in "The Labyrinth of Solitude."

OPPOSITE: In the carnival of Huejotzingo, Puebla, a dancer with a typical cardboard mask from Zacapoaxtla, and dress adorned with silky ribbons, waits for his turn to dance before La Morenita (the little dark-skinned Virgin).

OVERLEAF: Faith works miracles, and the trapeze artist seems to float above the tightrope facing the Basilica of Guadalupe, offering up his performance to the Virgin.

He left and felt sad	Salió, se fue triste,
because his message	porque no en seguida se cumplió
had not been fulfilled right away.	lo que era su mensaje.
He returned late on the same day	Después fue a regresar,
and went directly to the top of the hill	cuando ya se había completado el día,
and met Her,	allá se fue derecho
the Noble Lady from heaven,	a lo alto del cerrito.
where she was visible to him for the first time	Y llegó delante de ella,
and where she was awaiting him.	la noble señora celeste,
	allí donde la primera vez se le hizo visible,
	allí lo estaba aguardando.

ABOVE: "Moors and Christians," in the form of dancers, wait for their turn to perform. "This rite is about substituting the standards that govern Earth with those that govern the heavens," explains historian Alfonso Alfaro. "Art allows these Moors and Christians to emphasize their differences in order to overcome them."
OPPOSITE: A feather headdress decorated with the image of La Guadalupana and worn in the traditional dance of the "matachines" or "quetzalines" in the Totonaca area of Puebla and Veracruz.
OVERLEAF: "Concheros" from the Temple of the Cross, Querétaro, dance in front of the centuries-old basilica, holding the Virgin's standard high.

a popular vision

seeing Her,
bowing humbled before Her,
he said:
"My Noble Lady,
my Littlest Daughter, my dear Little Girl,
I did go
to where You sent me
to carry out Your dear breath,
Your dear word;
I also entered with difficulty the place where
the governing priest is.
I saw him,
I put Your breath, Your word before him
as You instructed me.
He received me with pleasure
and attention but he listened as if his
heart was not recognizing the truth.

He said:
'You will return, my son,
and I will listen to you more thoughtfully
and will contemplate from the beginning
why you have come,
what is your wish,
what is your will.'

I understood that
by the manner in which he replied
he truly believes
that Your wish for a temple
to be built for You here
was merely an invention of mine
and not an order that came from Your holy lips.

Y cuando así la vio,
ante ella se inclinó,
se humilló hasta el suelo,
le dijo:
Mi señora, señora, noble señora,
hija mía la más pequeña, mi muchachita,
ya fui allá,
a donde me enviaste como mensajero,
en verdad fui a que se cumpliera
tu reverenciado aliento, tu reverenciada palabra.
Aun cuando con mucha dificultad, entré,
allá donde es su lugar de estar,
del que manda a los sacerdotes,
en verdad lo vi,
en verdad ante él expuse
tu reverenciado aliento, tu reverenciada palabra,
como tú me lo mandaste.
Me recibió él con agrado,
y con atención escuchó
pero así me respondió
como que su corazón no lo reconoció,
no lo tuvo por verdad.

Me dijo:
Otra vez vendrás,
así despacio te escucharé,
así podré ver desde el comienzo
por qué has venido,
lo que es tu deseo,
lo que es tu voluntad.

De eso pude ver,
del modo como me respondió,
que en verdad piensa él
que tu reverenciada casa divina,
que quieres que aquí te hagan,
tal vez yo sólo la he inventado,
tal vez no viene de tus reverenciados labios.

In San Martín Tilcajete, in the state of Oaxaca, craftsman Vicente Hernández Vázquez
created this very personal and colorful Virgin in the same manner that the painted Oaxacan
"alebrijes" (animals hand-carved from pine wood) are made. (Óscar Reyes Collection)

47

For this reason I beg,
my Noble, Little Lady,
that You entrust the delivery
of Your message
to one of Your respected,
esteemed and well-known noblemen
so that he be believed.

For I am merely a wretched laborer,
a piece of rope,
a handbarrow,
a tail, a wing,
a man of no importance;
I myself need to be led
carried on someone's back,
that place you are sending me to is a place
where I am not used to going
or spending any time in, my Little Virgin,
my Youngest Daughter, my Lady, Little Girl.
Please excuse
the grief and displeasure
I cause Your heart, do not let wrath befall You,
Lady, my Lady."

Por esto, mucho te ruego,
señora mía, noble señora, mi muchachita,
que a alguno de los preciosos nobles,
los conocidos, reverenciados, honrados,
así le encargues
que lleve, que conduzca
tu reverenciado aliento, tu reverenciada palabra,
para que así sea creída.

En verdad yo soy un infeliz jornalero,
sólo soy como la cuerda de los cargadores,
en verdad soy parihuela,
sólo soy cola, soy ala,
soy llevado a cuestas, soy una carga,
en verdad no es lugar donde yo ando,
no es lugar donde yo me detengo,
allá a donde tú me envías,
mi muchachita, mi hija la más pequeña,
señora, noble señora.
Por favor, perdóname,
daré pena con esto a tu rostro, a tu corazón,
iré, caeré
en tu enojo, en tu cólera,
señora, señora mía.

ABOVE, LEFT: The Virgin of Guadalupe can be found in the depths of the sea, surrounded by fish, between Roqueta Island and Caleta beach in Acapulco, where glass-bottomed boats come close to her, entertaining the children on board.

ABOVE, RIGHT: A sculptor carves this very popular image in quarry stone.

OPPOSITE: The Virgin is set against a display of wooden fish, along with a mask carved in a coconut from Guerrero, in the famous Saturday Bazaar in San Ángel.

48

The perfect Blessed Virgin answered:
"Listen, my youngest son,
so that your heart may understand,
my servants
and messengers
are not people of importance;
those whom I can entrust
and those who can
fulfill my wish.
But it is necessary that you go
and champion this,
thanks to you my will
and my wish will be realized.
And I solemnly ask that
you go back tomorrow
and see the bishop.

Así le respondió la perfecta,
admirable doncella:
Escucha, tú el más pequeño de mis hijos,
que así lo comprenda tu corazón,
no son gente de rango mis servidores,
mis mensajeros,
a quienes yo podré encargar
que lleven mi aliento, mi palabra,
los que podrán hacer se cumpla mi voluntad.
Pero es muy necesario
que tú vayas,
abogues por esto,
gracias a ti se realice,
se cumpla mi querer, mi voluntad.
Y mucho te pido,
hijo mío, el más pequeño,
y mucho te mando
que, una vez más, vayas mañana,
vayas a ver al obispo.

ABOVE: Guadalupan images are very common on the roads that lead to Tepeyac.
OPPOSITE: The image appearing in this hologram picture changes according to the angle of the light. It represents the Virgin with her follower Juan Diego, as well as the Sacred Heart of Jesus.

TOP, LEFT: The Virgin in a frame of acrylic and wood with the four apparitions before Juan Diego.
TOP, RIGHT: "This home is Catholic." The Virgin with apparitions in gilt on paper.
CENTER AND ABOVE, RIGHT: Representations of the Virgin of painted clay made in the state of Mexico.
ABOVE, LEFT: Religious souvenirs for all tastes and budgets are sold in the Villa.

Go in my name,
and make known
that which is my wish,
that the sacred house
that I ask of him
be built and my will honored.
And again tell him that I,
in person,
the Eternal Virgin Holy Mary,
Mother of God Teotl,
send you as my messenger."

Juan Diego replied:
"My Noble Lady, my Child,
do not let me cause Your soul
grief.
I will wholeheartedly go
and fulfill Your mandate.
I will not abandon
nor consider strenuous the task.
I will go
and comply with Your wish,
although perhaps I will not be heard favorably;
or if I am heard,
perhaps I will not be believed.
Tomorrow afternoon,
after sunset,
I will solemnly come to bring
the bishop's response to Your request.
I leave You now, my Humblest Child,
my Little Child, Lady, Noble Lady,
so that You may rest."

III
He then left to go rest in his home.
And the following day,
Sunday, slightly before dawn
and still dark,
he left home
on his way to Tlatelolco
to be schooled in divine things
and to be present for roll call,
after which he would see the bishop.

Y de mi parte haz que sepa,
haz que oiga bien
lo que es mi querer,
lo que es mi voluntad,
para que cumpla,
edifique mi casa divina,
la que yo le pido.
Y, una vez más, bien dile
cómo yo,
la siempre doncella Santa María,
yo su madrecita de Teotl Dios,
a ti como mensajero te envío.

Y Juan Diego le respondió,
le dijo:
señora mía, noble señora, muchachita mía,
no disguste yo
a tu rostro, a tu corazón.
En verdad, de corazón iré,
marcharé para que se cumpla
tu reverenciado aliento, tu reverenciada palabra.
En verdad no lo abandonaré
ni tengo por penoso el camino.
Iré ya,
iré a cumplir tu voluntad,
sólo que tal vez no seré oído
y, si fuere escuchado,
quizá no seré creído.
Pero en verdad, mañana,
ya de tarde,
ya puesto el sol,
vendré a devolverte
tu reverenciado aliento, tu reverenciada palabra,
lo que me responderá
el que gobierna a los sacerdotes.
Ya te dejo, hija mía la más pequeña,
mi muchachita, señora, noble señora,
que así pues descanses.

III
Y luego él se fue a reposar a su casa.
Y ya el día siguiente,
domingo, todavía un poco de noche,
estaba oscuro,
de allá salió, de su casa,
vino derecho a Tlatelolco,
vino a aprender las cosas divinas
y a ser contado en la lista.
Luego ya verá al que gobierna a los sacerdotes.

And around ten o'clock	Y tal vez ya a las diez
everything had been taken care of:	había terminado,
Mass was over and roll had been called,	así ya había oído misa,
and the crowd had gone away.	y fue contado en la lista,
Juan Diego then went to the palace,	y toda la gente se había ido.
to the house of	Pero él, Juan Diego,
the governing bishop;	luego va al palacio,
And when he arrived	su casa, del que gobierna, obispo.
he put forth utmost persistence to see him,	Y cuando llegó,
and after much difficulty,	puso todo su empeño en verlo,
saw him once again.	y con mucha dificultad,
	otra vez lo vio.

TOP: Two Barbie dolls beside a small globe that lights up La Morenita of Tepeyac when plugged in.

ABOVE, LEFT: A candle is offered to ask for help with a difficult situation and is also used to express gratitude.

ABOVE, CENTER: Protective images painted on CDs for use in the car stereo.

ABOVE, RIGHT: A clay Virgin of Guerrero surrounded by lilies with a blue background and in a tin frame, created by Linda Palacios for her exhibition "La Luna Descalza."

OPPOSITE: Chief "conchero" dancer Ernesto, an important person in Mexican tradition and dance, plays the mandolin next to his altar in Mexico City.

He knelt at his feet.
He wept, he was sad
as he spoke to him,
as he revealed to him the word,
the breath of the Queen of Heaven.
Perhaps the message
or immaculate will of the Virgin
to build Her a sacred little house
where she proclaimed
or willed it to be
would not be believed.

Junto a sus pies se arrodilló.
Llora, se aflige, así le habla,
así le manifiesta
el reverenciado aliento, la reverenciada palabra,
de la noble señora celeste.
Acaso no será creído el mensaje,
la voluntad
de la que es en todo doncella,
que le hagan su casa divina
donde ella lo había dicho,
donde ella lo quería.

TOP, LEFT AND ABOVE, LEFT: Two versions of Guadalupe in the form of decorative metal objects.
ABOVE, RIGHT: The Virgin even appears on objects used in daily life such as this tray from Jalisco.
OPPOSITE: Two water carriers from Veracruz, mounted on a donkey, know that their valuable cargo
is blessed by the Virgin, as she appears on their containers.

But the governing bishop,	Mas el que gobierna, obispo,
inquired about many things	muchas cosas así le preguntó
to reassure himself,	e inquirió,
including where he had seen Her	para de este modo enterarse
and how she looked.	dónde la vio, cómo era.
He related everything to the bishop.	Todo se lo refirió al que gobierna, obispo.
But although his description	Pero, aunque todo se lo hizo manifiesto,
of Her and all that he had seen	cómo era y todo lo que vio,
and admired	lo que admiró,
was clear	que en verdad así aparece
and reflected Her as admirable and Ever-Virgin	la que es ella la en todo doncella,
Holy Mother of the Savior, Our Lord Jesus Christ,	la admirable, reverenciada madre,
he still did not fulfill Her wish.	del que nos liberó, Señor Nuestro Jesucristo,
	sin embargo, no luego se cumplió su deseo.

ABOVE: Everyday objects assume the wonder of Mexican icons: it is now fashionable to carry a Virgin shopping bag, or wear sequined earrings with the image of the Virgin on them. These two kinds of crafts are found in Puerto Vallarta.
OPPOSITE: Devotees of the Virgin use modern scapulars (on which other images appear) for protection from illness, purgatory, and the flames of hell.
OVERLEAF: Popular T-shirts emblazoned with the images of Christ, Guadalupe, the pope, and Saint Jude are just as popular as those with pop music groups like Los Temerarios and the "norteño" group Límite.

The bishop said that the petition brought
by Juan Diego would not be carried out
based solely on his word,
and that some sign would still be necessary
so that it could be well believed
as to why he was sent as messenger
by the Noble Heavenly Lady.

Thus Juan Diego listened,
and later said to the bishop:
"My Lord, he who governs,
what would be the sign that you ask for;
I will earnestly go
and ask the Noble Heavenly Lady
who sent me
for a sign."

The bishop saw
that he held everything to be true
because he did not doubt anything nor hesitate,
and then he dismissed him.

Dijo el obispo que no sólo por la palabra,
la petición de él, Juan Diego, se hará
se cumplirá lo que pidió.
Todavía se necesitaba alguna señal
para que bien pudiera ser creído
cómo a él lo enviaba como mensajero
la noble señora celeste.

Y así que lo escuchó Juan Diego,
luego le dijo al obispo:
señor, tú que gobiernas,
mira cuál será
la señal que tú pides,
que en verdad iré luego,
iré a pedírsela a la noble señora celeste,
la que a mí me envió.

Y como vio el obispo
que él tenía ello por verdad,
porque en nada dudaba, vacilaba,
luego lo hizo irse.

ABOVE: In La Nueva Bonampak, Martha and Eduardo make tortillas under the protection of the
Virgin of Guadalupe.
OPPOSITE: Delicious jello is sold on the docks of Acapulco from an ice box adorned with the beloved icon.

ANDREA
9 AÑOS CAballero

Doy las gracias
a la virgencita de
GUADALUPE POR QUE
Mi IDOLO EL SANTO GANO UN[...]
A LUCHA IMPORTANTE CONTRA [...]
BLU DEMON. SANDRA MORA [...]

And when he left,
the bishop immediately
ordered some members of his household
whom he trusted well
to follow him,
to see where he went,
who he saw,
and with whom he spoke.

And so it was done.
And Juan Diego continued on at once.
But those who followed him
lost sight of him
after crossing the wood-plank bridge
at the ravine
next to Tepeyac.

Y cuando ya se va,
en seguida manda el obispo
a algunas de las gentes de su casa,
en las que bien confía,
que lo vayan a seguir,
que vean bien hacia dónde va,
y a quién mira,
con quién habla.

Así se hizo.
Y Juan Diego en seguida se fue derecho,
siguió la calzada.
Pero los que iban tras él,
allá donde se abre la barranca,
junto al Tepeyac,
en el puente de tablas,
vinieron a perderlo.

ABOVE: "Ex voto" is a Latin word meaning "by promise." Objects that have been promised to God, the Virgin or to saints to ask for something or acknowledge a miracle, are hung in churches or sanctuaries, and form an important part of an old and popular Mexican tradition. This painting on copperplate explains the occurrence of a "miracle"—in this case, a wrestler winning a match—and expresses gratitude to the Virgin.
OPPOSITE: This drawing made by the young Andrea Caballero seems to confirm that Guadalupan passion is in Mexicans' blood.

Although they searched everywhere,
Juan Diego couldn't be seen anywhere.
Thus they returned,
not only because they were tired,
but because they were disgusted
and angry.

And so they went to tell the governing bishop;
they went to convince him
not to believe Juan Diego;
they told the bishop that he was lying,
that he merely invented
what he had come and confessed
or that he simply dreamed up
what he had said and asked for.
Thus they declared that
if he returned
they would then trap him
and capture him
so he wouldn't lie again
and cause disorder unto the people.

Aunque por todas partes lo buscaron,
en ninguna parte lo vieron.
Así vinieron a regresarse,
no sólo porque con esto mucho se cansaron,
sino también porque él los disgustó,
les causó enojo.

Así fueron a decírselo al que gobierna, obispo.
Le fueron a exponer que no le creyera,
le dijeron que sólo contaba mentiras,
sólo inventaba eso que venía a decirle,
o que sólo soñó,
sólo sacó del sueño,
eso que le decía,
eso que le pedía.
Y así dijeron que,
si una vez más venía,
regresaba,
luego lo atraparían
y con fuerza lo apresarían,
para que ya no otra vez mintiera,
inquietara a la gente.

ABOVE: The driver of one of these two collided buses painted this panel for the Virgin to show that most of the passengers came out miraculously unscathed. (Museum of the Basilica of Guadalupe Collection, Mexico City)
OPPOSITE: The offering of a girl who prays to the Virgin for the gift of a little brother. (Museum of the Basilica of Guadalupe Collection, Mexico City)
OVERLEAF: The victim of an assault acknowledges Saint Anthony and the Virgin for having saved his life. (Museum of the Basilica of Guadalupe Collection, Mexico City)

The following day, Monday,
when Juan Diego had to carry
some sign so as to ensure that he would be believed,
he never returned.
Because when he approached his house,
one of his uncles by the name of Juan Bernardino
became ill,
and was on the verge of death.
He even went to call the doctor
who took care of him,
but it was too late,
for he was very ill.
And then at nighttime,
his uncle begged for Juan Diego
to leave at dawn when it was still dark,
and call one of the priests
from Tlatelolco
to come and hear his confession
and prepare him for his demise.
Because it was in his heart
that it was indeed his time,
and that he would then die,
because he would no longer rise,
he would not be cured.

And Tuesday,
when it was still very dark,
Juan Diego left his house
to call the priest
in Tlatelolco.
And he approached the little summit,
at the foot of Tepeyac,
where the road leads
to where the sun sets,
over where it once emerged.
He said:
If I continue on this road,
lest the Noble Little Lady not come to see me,
because she will stall me like before
and have me deliver the signal
to the governing bishop
as she has ordered me to.
But first our suffering must end,
and I must call the priest
because my poor uncle
anxiously awaits him.

El día siguiente, lunes,
cuando tenía que llevar Juan Diego
alguna señal para ser creído,
no vino a regresar.
Porque, cuando fue a acercarse a su casa,
a un tío suyo, de nombre Juan Bernardino,
se le puso la enfermedad,
ya estaba al cabo.
Aún fue a llamar al médico,
todavía se ocupó de él,
pero ya no era tiempo,
pues ya estaba al cabo.
Y cuando ya era de noche,
le rogó su tío que todavía de madrugada,
aún a oscuras, saliera,
fuera a llamar allá en Tlatelolco,
a alguno de los sacerdotes,
para que viniera a confesarlo
y a dejarlo preparado.
Porque eso ya estaba en su corazón,
que en verdad ya era tiempo,
que ya entonces moriría,
porque ya no se levantaría,
ya no sanaría.

Y el martes,
cuando todavía estaba muy oscuro,
entonces salió de su casa Juan Diego,
llamará al sacerdote
allá en Tlatelolco.
Y vino a acercarse al cerrito,
al pie del Tepeyac,
donde sale el camino
hacia donde se pone el sol,
por allá donde antes había salido.
Dijo:
Si sigo derecho el camino,
no sea que venga a verme la noble señora,
porque me detendrá como antes,
para que lleve la señal
al sacerdote que gobierna,
según me lo ordenó.
Que antes nos deje nuestra aflicción,
que así llame yo al sacerdote
al que el pobre de mi tío
nada más está aguardando.

Detail on the facade of a house in the neighborhood of Tizapán, San Ángel, Mexico City inspired by
van Gogh's "Starry Night." The image of the Virgin was created using pieces of tile. The owner of the
house is a hairdresser who admires the Dutch painter and is devoted to Guadalupe.

Then he turned toward the hill,	Luego rodeó al cerro,
climbed up its center, where,	por en medio subió y de allí,
on one side,	por una parte,
he passed by where the sun rises.	vino a pasar hacia donde sale el sol.
He moved quickly on his way to Mexico City,	Así, de prisa, iba a acercarse a México,
so that the Noble Heavenly Lady	así no lo detendría
would not detain him.	la noble señora celeste.
He thought that where he turned	Piensa él que allí donde dio vuelta
she who sees everything	no podrá verlo
would not be able to see him.	la que bien a todas partes ve.

ABOVE: A quarry-stone and "tezontle" volcanic-rock street icon (LEFT), a niche arranged out of the same volcanic rock (ABOVE, RIGHT), and another altar made of decorated tile in Tepoztlán, Morelos (TOP, RIGHT).

OPPOSITE: An altar dedicated to the Virgin on Aguacate Street in the neighborhood of Coyoacán in Mexico City. It has become common to place her image on street corners to avoid trash bags being left there.

He contemplated how it was that She descended
from the summit of the little hill.
She had been watching him from there,
from where She had seen him before.
She came to meet him
on one side of the hill,
She came to block his way,
and She said:
"Where are you going,
where are you headed,
my youngest son?"

But perhaps he became a little upset?
Or maybe he was ashamed?
Or perhaps he got scared, became frightened?
He bowed down to Her,
he greeted Her, he said:
"My Little Maiden, my Smallest Daughter,
Noble Lady, I hope You are happy;
how are You this morning?
Does Your beloved little body feel well,
my Lady, my Honorable Daughter?
I will cause Your face and Your heart anguish,
do You know, my Little Girl,
that a servant of Yours, my uncle,
is on the verge of death?
An acute illness has infected him,
and the truth is that he will soon die of it.
And now I shall go quickly
to Your honorable house in Mexico City,
I will call one of the priests
of our beloved Lord
to hear my uncle's confession
and to prepare him,
because we were undoubtedly born for that reason,
we have come to wait
for the labor of our death.
But if I am going to do this,
I will later return here.
Thus I will go,
I will carry
Your revered breath, Your honored word,
Lady, my Little Girl.

Contempló él cómo vino a descender ella
de la cumbre del cerrito.
Desde allí lo había estado mirando,
desde allí donde antes lo vio.
Vino a encontrarse con él
a un costado del cerro,
vino a atajarlo,
le dijo:
Hijo mío el más pequeño,
¿a dónde vas,
a dónde te encaminas?

Pero él, ¿acaso un poco se perturbó?
¿O acaso tuvo vergüenza?
¿O tal vez se asustó, se espantó?
Ante ella se postró,
la saludó, le dijo:
Muchachita mía, hija mía la más pequeña,
noble señora, que estés contenta,
¿cómo te amaneció?
¿Sientes bien tu precioso cuerpecito,
señora mía, reverenciada hija mía?
Daré aflicción a tu rostro, a tu corazón.
Sabe, muchachita mía,
que está ya al cabo
un servidor tuyo, mi tío.
Grave enfermedad se le ha puesto,
porque en verdad por ella pronto morirá.
Y así pues, me iré con prisa
a tu reverenciada casa de México,
llamaré a uno de los amados del Señor Nuestro,
a uno de nuestros sacerdotes,
que vaya a confesarlo
y a dejarlo preparado,
porque en verdad para esto nacimos,
hemos venido a esperar
el trabajo de nuestra muerte.
Pero si voy a hacer esto,
luego otra vez volveré acá.
Así iré,
llevaré
tu reverenciado aliento, tu reverenciada palabra,
señora, muchachita mía.

OPPOSITE: A stand with candles and lamps for keeping devotion alive in the home in the San Juan Market in Mexico City.
OVERLEAF: On an appetizing fruit stand is the image of the Guadalupan queen on a support of jicama, watermelon, coconut, and cucumber.

ABOVE: The image of the Virgin is always present in Mexican herbal markets, where all types of "miracles" are expected to be found: attaining an ideal weight or gaining sexual prowess.
OPPOSITE: Placed on top of a television set, the Virgin also dominates entertainment. On television, actress Carmen Salinas hosts a show that explores a common complaint, "My husband doesn't satisfy me and I can't bear it anymore!"

ABOVE, LEFT: A Day of the Dead altar in the Urquiza studio with lilies, marigolds, and cut tissue paper is a reminder of Posada, the artist.

ABOVE, RIGHT: A poignant altar placed at the base of the destroyed Twin Towers after the tragedy of September 11, 2001.

OPPOSITE: A spectacular altar for the departed erected in the home of photographer and artist Lourdes Almeida. It is decorated with various representations of death, "papel picado" (cut tissue paper), and objects that the deceased liked.

Forgive me,
be patient with me a little longer,
because I am not ridiculing You,
my Youngest Daughter,
my Little Girl, I will come quickly tomorrow morning."

Thus when she heard
Juan Diego's word
the altogether merciful
Virgin replied:
"Listen,
so that it may remain in your heart,
my youngest son,
what frightened you,
what afflicted you is nothing.
Do not let it disturb
your face, your heart,
do not fear this or any other distressing
or burdensome illness.
Am I not here,
I, who am your mother?
Are you not in my shadow
and under my protection?
Am I not the reason for your happiness?
Are you not in my lap,
where I protect you?
Perhaps there is something more that you need?
Do not grieve
nor be disturbed by anything,
do not be afflicted by
the illness of your uncle.
He will not die now of his illness.
Be assured that he has been cured of it."

And then his uncle was cured,
as it was later learned.
And upon hearing
the revered breath, the honored word
of the Noble Heavenly Lady,
Juan Diego was greatly consoled
and his heart became peaceful.
And then he begged
to be sent as messenger
to see the governing bishop,
and to send a sign or proof
so that he might be believed.

Perdóname,
todavía tenme paciencia,
porque no me burlo de ti,
hija mía, la más pequeña,
hijita mía, mañana mismo vendré de prisa.

Así que oyó
la palabra de Juan Diego
le respondió la compasiva,
del todo doncella:
Escucha,
que así esté en tu corazón,
hijo mío, el más pequeño,
nada es lo que te hace temer,
lo que te aflige.
Que no se perturbe
tu rostro, tu corazón,
no temas esta enfermedad
ni otra cualquier enfermedad,
que aflige, que agobia.
¿Acaso no estoy aquí,
yo que soy tu madrecita?
¿Acaso no estás bajo mi sombra,
y en resguardo?
¿Acaso no soy la razón de tu alegría?
¿No estás en mi regazo,
en donde yo te protejo?
¿Acaso todavía te hace falta algo?
Que ya no te aflija cosa alguna,
que no te inquiete,
que no te acongoje
la enfermedad de tu tío.
En verdad no morirá ahora por ella.
Esté en tu corazón que él ya sanó.

Y luego entonces se curó su tío,
como así luego se supo.
Y Juan Diego, al escuchar
el reverenciado aliento, la reverenciada palabra
de la noble señora celeste,
mucho se tranquilizó en su corazón,
su corazón se calmó.
Y le rogó entonces
que lo enviara como mensajero,
para que viera al que gobierna, obispo,
y le llevara su señal, su testimonio,
para que él le crea.

A satin banner carefully embroidered for the annual pilgrimage from Villa Victoria in the
state of Mexico to Tepeyac.

And the Noble Heavenly Lady	Y la noble señora celeste
later ordered him	luego le ordenó
to climb to the summit of the little hill,	que subiera a la cumbre del cerrito,
where he had seen Her before.	allí donde él la había visto antes.
She said to him:	Le dijo:
"Climb, my youngest son,	Sube, tú el más pequeño de mis hijos,
to the top of the hill	a la cumbre del cerrito
and where you saw me	y allí donde tú me viste
and where I gave you orders,	y donde te di mi mandato,
there you will see	allí verás
assorted flowers spread about.	extendidas flores variadas.
Cut them, gather them,	Córtalas, júntalas,
assemble them,	ponlas todas juntas,
then come right away	baja en seguida,
and bring them before my presence."	tráelas aquí delante de mí.

ABOVE, LEFT: A neatly embroidered flag belonging to cyclists from Loma del Lienzo and Cuadrilla Vieja in the state of Mexico used on the annual pilgrimage.

TOP, RIGHT: This Guadalupan image was painted with acrylic on bright pink tissue paper by the great craftsman and artist of Mexico City Enrique Ávila.

ABOVE, RIGHT: Swallows, stars, and roses frame the Virgin of Guadalupe.

OPPOSITE: Women pilgrims arrive at the Villa with cloth-painted banners that represent "La Patrona," the female patron saint, who is loved by people from all social classes.

OVERLEAF: An arch decorated with images made of seeds in the atrium of the chapel in the Guadalupe barrio of Malinalco, in the state of Mexico, for the December 12th celebration.

These four popular images are made of cloth embroidered with sequins, "chaquira" beads, and glitter. The repetition of the basic image is reminiscent of Andy Warhol's work.

And later Juan Diego	Y luego Juan Diego
climbed the little hill	subió al cerrito
and when he arrived at the top,	y cuando llegó a su cumbre,
he was amazed	mucho se maravilló
that so many varieties of flowers,	de cuántas flores allí se extendían,
like those of Castile, were blooming,	tenían abiertas sus corolas,
long before the time that they were to bud,	variadas flores preciosas, como las de Castilla,
because, being out of season,	no siendo aún su tiempo de darse.
they would freeze over.	Porque era entonces
The flowers were very fragrant	cuando arreciaba el hielo.
and covered with dewdrops from the night,	Las flores eran muy olorosas,
they looked like precious pearls.	eran como perlas preciosas,
He promptly began to cut them	henchidas del rocío de la noche.
and gathered them	En seguida comenzó a cortarlas,
in the hollow of his "tilma."	todas las vino a juntar
	en el hueco de su tilma.

ABOVE: Always full of light, the Queen of Mexico elaborated in beads (ABOVE, LEFT), surrounded by little lights (TOP, LEFT), and placed even in front of McDonalds, next to the Mexican flag (ABOVE, RIGHT).

90

But the hilltop
was no place for flowers to grow,
because it is rocky and
there are thistles, thorny plants,
patches of prickly pear, and an abundance of mesquite trees.
And although some weeds would grow,
it was during the month of December
when all vegetation
would be destroyed by frost.

Pero allá en la cumbre del cerrito
no se daban ningunas flores,
porque es pedregoso,
hay abrojos, plantas con espinas,
nopaleras, abundancia de mezquites.
Y si algunas hierbas pequeñas allá se dan,
entonces en el mes de diciembre
todo lo come,
lo echa a perder el hielo.

TOP, LEFT AND ABOVE, LEFT: More popular images with the national flag, flowers, sequins, and glitter.
ABOVE, RIGHT: A blue light illuminates the devotion of Juan Diego to the Virgin in this gold-framed piece.
OVERLEAF: Images placed in the plaza of the Villa on December 12th. Everyone gets a souvenir.

And then he came down	Y luego vino a bajar,
to bring the Noble Heavenly Lady	vino a traerle a la noble señora celeste
the different flowers that he had gone to cut.	las variadas flores que había ido a cortar.
And when she saw them	Y cuando ella las vio,
she took them with Her precious hands.	con sus reverenciadas manos las cogió.
Then she put them again all together	Luego las puso de nuevo
into the hollow of his "tilma,"	en el hueco de la tilma de Juan Diego,
and said to him:	y le dijo:
"My son, my youngest son,	Hijo mío, el más pequeño,
these different flowers are proof,	estas variadas flores son la prueba,
the sign that you will take to the bishop.	la señal que llevarás al obispo.
You will tell him on my behalf	De parte mía le dirás
that with these, he see my will	que con esto vea lo que es mi voluntad
and that with these, my will be done,	y que con esto cumpla mi querer,
which is my desire.	lo que es mi deseo.
And you, you are my messenger,	Y tú, tú eres mi mensajero,
the trust is in you.	en ti está la confianza.
And so I strongly urge you	Y bien yo mucho te ordeno
That before the bishop,	que únicamente a solas, ante el obispo,
alone and in private,	extiendas tu tilma
you open your "tilma"	y le muestres lo que llevas.
and show him what you bring.	Y todo le referirás,
And you will tell him everything,	le dirás cómo te ordené
You will tell him how I ordered you	que subieras a la cumbre del cerrito,
To go up the summit of the hill,	fueras a cortar las flores
to cut the flowers	y todo lo que tú viste,
and all that you saw,	lo que tú admiraste.
all that you admired.	Así tú convencerás en su corazón
Thus you will convince him in his soul,	al que es gobernante de los sacerdotes,
the governor of priests,	así luego él dispondrá
and he will arrange	que se haga,
that the divine house I had asked for	se levante mi casa divina,
be raised."	la que le he pedido.

"Papaya, Orange and Rain II," a representation of the Virgin done by the Monterrey artist Silvia Ordóñez in 1993. Oil on canvas, 4'6" x 5'3".

IV

And the Noble Heavenly Lady
delivered Her order.
He went directly
to the road of Mexico City,
being happy
and his heart calm
believing it would turn out well,
he would rightly take the flowers,
taking great care
of what was inside the hollow of his "tilma,"
lest something should fall.
The aroma of the different
precious flowers delighted him.

When he arrived
at the bishop's palace
he was discovered by the caretaker
and the other servants of this governing bishop.
He asked that they tell the bishop
that he wished to see him,
but nobody wanted to.
They did not want to listen to him
perhaps because it was still early, at the break of dawn.
Maybe they recognized him,
or that the way he hung about
bothered them.
And those fellow priests who had lost sight of him
had already spoken to him
when they went to follow him.

IV

Y cuando ya le dio su orden
la noble señora celeste,
vino él siguiendo en derechura
la calzada de México,
ya está contento,
ya está calmado su corazón,
porque va a salir bien,
bien llevará las flores.
Va cuidando mucho
lo que viene en el hueco de su tilma,
no sea que algo se le caiga.
Lo alegra el aroma
de las variadas flores preciosas.

Cuando llegó
al palacio del obispo,
lo fueron a encontrar el que cuida su casa
y los otros servidores del sacerdote que gobierna.
Él les pidió que le dijeran
que quería él verlo,
pero ninguno de ellos quiso.
No querían escucharlo
o quizás era aún de madrugada.
O tal vez ya lo reconocían,
sólo los molestaba,
como que se les colgaba.
Y ya les habían hablado sus compañeros,
los que fueron a perderlo de vista
cuando habían ido a seguirlo.

ABOVE: "The Miracle of Tepeyac, V," 2001, a piece by Ricardo Serrano Cornejo, Mexico City. Digital graphics on paper, 3 1/2 x 5 7/8". (Courtesy of the IX Guadalupan Biennial, Universidad Autónoma Metropolitana) The artist used the label of a popular soap for his composition.
OPPOSITE: Virgin of wax and cloth, by Jeffrey Vallance. (Tijuana Wax Museum. Courtesy of the Installation Gallery. Insite 2000, E.V.A.)

Retablo de Ntra. Señora Guadalupe Tonantzin

ABOVE: "Juan Diego and the Virgin," 2002, Carmen Parra, Mexico City. Pastel and pencil on paper, 3'3" x 2'3". Parra is famous for her religion-inspired works.
OPPOSITE: "Altarpiece of Our Lady of Guadalupe-Tonantzin," 1971, Jaime Saldívar, Mexico City. Oil on canvas, 6'6" x 4'3". (Courtesy Club de Industriales)

For a long time
he awaited the bishop's decision.
And they saw that
he stood there for quite some time
with his head down,
without doing anything,
in case he were to be called.
And since it seemed that he carried something
in the hollow of his "tilma,"
they later approached him
to see what he was holding
and in that way, satisfy their curiosity.

And Juan Diego saw
that he could not hide
what he was carrying from them,
and because of this they upset him,
they shoved
or perhaps hit him,
and he showed them that they were flowers.
And upon seeing
all the different flowers like the ones from Castile,
and since it wasn't yet time for them to bloom
they greatly admired
that they were still quite fresh,
with their open corollas
their fragrance simply beautiful.

So they wished
to take a few of them.
They dared to take them
three times
although nothing really happened;
because when they tried to do so
they no longer could see the flowers;
what they saw inside the "tilma"
was rather something resembling
painting or embroidery,
or something that was sewn.

Por largo tiempo
estuvo él esperando la palabra.
Y vieron ellos que mucho tiempo
allí estuvo de pie,
estuvo con la cabeza baja,
estuvo sin hacer nada,
por si tal vez fuera llamado.
Y como que venía trayendo algo
que estaba en el hueco de su tilma,
luego ya se le acercaron,
para ver qué es lo que traía
y satisfacer así su corazón.

Y vio Juan Diego
que no podía ocultarles
eso que llevaba,
y por ello lo afligirían,
le darían de empellones,
o tal vez lo golpearían,
un poco les mostró que eran flores.
Y al ver que todas
eran variadas flores como las de Castilla,
y como no era tiempo de que se dieran,
mucho se admiraron
de que estaban muy frescas,
con sus corolas abiertas,
así olorosas, preciosas.

Y tuvieron deseo
de coger algunas pocas,
sacarlas.
Y tres veces fue
que se atrevieron a tomarlas,
aunque nada realmente sucedió.
Porque cuando trataban de hacerlo,
ya no veían las flores,
sólo como una pintura o un bordado,
o algo que estuviera cosido,
así lo veían en la tilma.

Our Lady of the Auditorium. Behind the scenes in many theaters in Mexico, the protective image of Guadalupe keeps vigil; dancers, singers, and actors make the sign of the cross and entrust themselves to her before their performance. This altar, over eight feet tall, is by the recognized artisan Rafael Álvarez.

They immediately went to tell	En seguida fueron a decirle
the governing bishop	al que gobierna, obispo,
what they had seen	lo que habían contemplado,
and how the little man who had come before	y cómo quería verlo
wanted to see him again	el hombrecillo que otras veces había venido,
and that he had been waiting	y que ya llevaba largo rato
a long time for a decision and	en espera de la palabra
hence wanted to see him.	pues quería verlo.
And as soon as the governing bishop	Y el que gobierna, obispo,
heard this,	así como escuchó esto,
and understood in his heart	tuvo ya en su corazón
that this was the sign	que ésa era su señal,
that he wanted to bring near to his heart,	con la que quería acercarse a su corazón,
so he could carry out	para que él llevara a cabo
the task that the little man had requested.	el encargo en que andaba el hombrecillo.

ABOVE, LEFT: "In Her Most Recent Apparition," 1998, María Sada, Mexico City. Oil and gold and silver leaf on copper laminate, 14 ¹/₈ x 11". An ingenious piece that represents the Virgin in a theater: a public appearance, hence the title.

ABOVE, RIGHT: "Virgin II," 2001, Mónica Mayer, Mexico City. Digital graphics on paper, 5 ¹/₂ x 7 ¹/₂". (Courtesy of the IX Guadalupan Biennial, Universidad Autónoma Metropolitana) "This is you or me, the archetype of the mother, and Guadalupe as the most visible representative in our culture. I seek to adopt her positive aspects and add others that are closer to the actual reality of women," Mayer comments.

OPPOSITE: "Tattooed Car III," 1997, Betsabeé Romero, Mexico City. Tattoo on goat skin of the Aztec serpent with the "Catrina" of the Posada at its feet, 2'7" x 1'2" x 1'4".

OVERLEAF, LEFT: Untitled, 2001, Igancio Vera Ponce, Zacatecas. Etched plate on paper and watercolor, 8 ¹/₂ x 11". (Courtesy of the IX Guadalupan Biennial, Universidad Autónoma Metropolitana)

OVERLEAF, RIGHT: "Zapatist Virgin," 2001, Antonio Platas, Mexico City. Digital print on paper, 6 ³/₄ x 4 ¹/₄". (Courtesy of the IX Guadalupan Biennial, Universidad Autónoma Metropolitana)

The bishop then ordered
that he enter as he would then see him.
So he entered and kneeled before him,
as he had done before.
And once again he told him
of all that he had seen
all that he had admired and of his message.

He said:
"My Lord, you who govern,
in truth, I did so,
I carried out your order.
I went to tell the Lady, my Lady,
Noble Heavenly Lady, Saint Mary,
precious Mother of God,
that you asked for a sign
in order to believe me,
and in that way you would build
Her sacred little house
there, where She asked
you to build it.
And I told Her
that I had given you my word,
that I would bring you a sign,
a testimony of Her revered will.
And She accepted your request with joy,
Her sign,
the testimony to carry out;
to fulfill Her will.

And still today, at nighttime,
She ordered me once again
to come and see you.
And I asked Her for the proof
so that I could be believed,
as she said that She would give it to me,
and She kept her promise immediately.

And she sent me to the summit
of the little hill, where I had seen Her before,
so that I could cut
the flowers like those from Castile.
And I went to cut them,
and later carried them down the hill.

Luego ordenó
que entrara, lo verá.
Y entró, se inclinó ante él,
como antes lo había hecho.
Y una vez más le refirió
todo lo que había visto,
lo que había admirado y su mensaje.

Le dijo:
señor mío, tú que gobiernas,
en verdad ya hice,
ya cumplí según tú me ordenaste.
Así fui a decirle a la señora, mi señora,
la noble señora celeste, Santa María,
su preciosa madrecita de Dios,
que tú pedías una señal
para creerme,
así le harías su casa divina
allá donde ella te pedía
que la construyeras.
Y le dije
que yo te había dado mi palabra
de que te traería alguna señal,
un testimonio de su reverenciada voluntad,
según en mi mano tú lo dejaste.
Y ella escuchó bien
tu reverenciado aliento, tu reverenciada palabra,
y recibió con alegría lo que tú pedías,
la señal suya,
el testimonio para que se haga,
se cumpla su voluntad.

Y hoy, todavía de nochecita,
me ordenó que, una vez más,
viniera a verte.
Y yo le pedí su señal
para ser creído,
como me dijo que me la daría,
y en seguida lo cumplió.

Y me envió a la cumbre del cerrito,
en donde antes yo la vi,
para que allí cortara
flores como las de Castilla.
Y yo las fui a cortar,
las llevé luego abajo.

"Guadalupe, Eyes of Love," 2001, Harryson De Carli Testa, Brazil. Acrylic ink with chalk and pastel on paper, 11 x 7 ½". (Courtesy of the IX Guadalupan Biennial, Universidad Autónoma Metropolitana)

And she picked them up
with Her revered hands.
Later she put them
in the hollow of my 'tilma'
so that I could deliver them to you.

Even though I knew
that the summit of the little hill
is not a place that grows flowers
because it is rocky,
with thistles and thorny plants,
wild prickly pear, and mesquite trees,
I did not doubt nor hesitate
because of this.

Y ella con sus reverenciadas manos las cogió.
Luego las puso en el hueco de mi tilma,
para que a ti te las trajera,
te las viniera a entregar.

Aunque yo sabía
que no es lugar donde se dan las flores
la cumbre del cerrito,
porque sólo es pedregoso,
hay abrojos, plantas espinosas,
nopales silvestres, mezquites,
no por esto dudé,
no por esto titubeé.

"Seven Apparitions," 2002, Magali Ávila, Mexico City. Encaustic and oil on wood, 3'3" x 3'3".
The tones of the painting are purple, a color considered to be the most spiritual.

108

I approached the summit of the little hill;	Fui a acercarme a la cumbre del cerrito,
I saw that it was the Earth covered in flowers,	vi que era la Tierra florida,
with different flowers sprouting	allí habían brotado variadas flores,
like the roses from Castile,	como las rosas de Castilla,
resplendent with dew,	resplandecientes de rocío,
then I went to cut them.	así luego las fui a cortar.
And she ordered me	Y me dijo ella
to give them to you on Her behalf,	que de parte suya te las diera,
so that way I may fulfill	y así yo cumpliría
the sign that you ask for	para que tú vieras
so that you may see.	la señal que pides.
And you may fulfill	De este modo cumplirás
Her revered will	lo que es su reverenciada voluntad
and thus my word, my message	y así aparezca es verdad
may prove to be true.	mi palabra, mi mensaje.
Here they are, accept them."	Aquí están, recíbelas.

ABOVE: "Disappearances in the Valley and some Stolen Angels II," 1995, Betsabeé Romero, Mexico City. Oil on cloth, wood, dried flowers, and glass, 5'6" x 7'4". Romero cautions us to take care of the valley of Mexico, so that it does not disappear amid so much contamination, or the Virgin may also go...

OVERLEAF: "Guadalupe in the Clouds," 2002, Eric Giebeler. Flying above Mexican land, the photographer's trained eye captured an "apparition" for this photomontage.

Then he held out his white "tilma,"
the hollow of which held the flowers.
And as the different flowers, like those from Castile,
fell to the floor,
there on his "tilma" remained the sign,
the precious image appeared
of the wholly Blessed Virgin Mary,
Mother of God,
just as she is found today,
there she is kept now,
in Her beloved little house
in Her sacred little house,
in Tepeyac, which is called Guadalupe.

And when the governing bishop
and all those who were present saw the image,
they fell to their knees and greatly admired Her.
Then they stood up to see Her,
and they were moved, their hearts touched,
as if she had uplifted their souls and their minds.

And with tears and repentance
the governing bishop
begged Juan Diego to forgive him
for not having then fulfilled
Her revered will,
Her holy word.
And the bishop rose
and untied the collar from which hung
the clothing, Juan Diego's "tilma"
on which the revered sign appeared.
Then he took it and
placed it in the oratory.

Y extendió luego su blanca tilma
en cuyo hueco estaban las flores.
Y al caer al suelo
las variadas flores como las de Castilla,
allí en su tilma quedó la señal,
apareció la preciosa imagen
de la en todo doncella Santa María,
su madrecita de Dios,
tal como hoy se halla,
allí ahora se guarda,
en su preciosa casita,
en su templecito,
en Tepeyac, donde se dice Guadalupe.

Y cuando la contempló el que gobierna, obispo,
y también todos los que allí estaban,
se arrodillaron, mucho la admiraron.
se levantaron para verla,
se conmovieron, se afligió su corazón,
como que se elevó su corazón, su pensamiento.

Y el que gobierna, obispo,
con lágrimas, con pesar,
le suplicó,
le pidió lo perdonara
por no haber cumplido luego
su reverenciada voluntad,
su reverenciado aliento, su reverenciada palabra.
Y el obispo se levantó,
desató del cuello, de donde estaba colgada,
la vestidura, la tilma de Juan Diego,
en la que se mostró,
en donde se volvió reverenciada señal
la noble señora celeste.
Y luego la llevó allá,
fue a colocarla en su oratorio.

Religious images are even present in computers.

And Juan Diego
stayed at the house of the bishop
for an entire day.
And the next day the bishop said to him:
"Go so that you may show
the location of the revered will
of the Noble Heavenly Lady
so that Her chapel may be erected."

Y allí todavía un día entero
estuvo Juan Diego,
en la casa del obispo,
quien hizo se quedara allí.
Y al día siguiente, le dijo:
Anda, para que tú muestres
dónde es la reverenciada voluntad
de la noble señora celeste
que se le levante su templo.

ABOVE: Sones Jarochos during the beatification of the martyrs of Oaxaca, Juan Bautista, and Jacinto de Los Angeles, August 10, 2002.
OPPOSITE: No soccer player, actor, or politician brings together as many people as the Pope John Paul II. They say that more than eight million people greeted him on his trip from the papal nunciature to the Basilica of Guadalupe and back. More than 80 percent of television sets were tuned in to watch. This image, highlighted with glitter, unites three figures to celebrate the canonization of Juan Diego on July 31, 2002.
OVERLEAF: Two great Mexican favorites side by side: the personification of soccer represented by the American eagle, stepping on the Chivas of Guadalajara and Pope John Paul II with Juan Diego, the first indigenous saint.

CANONIZACION 2002

SAN JUAN DIEGO

Immediately an order was given
that the chapel be erected.
But Juan Diego, after he had shown
where the Noble Heavenly Lady
had ordered
that Her sacred little house be built,
declared
that he wanted to go home
to see his uncle Bernardino,
who was found to be quite ill when he had left;
and he had gone to call one of the priests
in Tlatelolco,
to give him confession
and to prepare him,
his uncle, whom the Noble Heavenly Lady
said was already cured.

And not only did they allow him to leave,
but they also accompanied him to his house.
When they arrived,
they saw the revered uncle
very well,
with nothing afflicting him.
He marveled that his nephew
should arrive accompanied
by many dignified people.
He asked his nephew
what had happened
for him to be so honored.

And he responded
that when he went there
to call for a priest
to grant him confession and to prepare his uncle
in Tepeyac,
the Noble Heavenly Lady had appeared to him
and sent him to Mexico City
to see the governing bishop
and ordered that Her house be built in Tepeyac
and ordered him not to worry
because his uncle was already cured,
and with that his heart was appeased.

En seguida se dio orden
de hacerla, levantarla.
Pero Juan Diego cuando ya mostró
dónde había ordenado
la noble señora celeste
que se le levantara su templo,
luego manifestó
que quería acercarse a su casa,
ir a ver a su tío Bernardino,
que se hallaba muy mal cuando lo dejó,
y había ido a llamar a uno de los sacerdotes,
allá a Tlatelolco,
para que lo confesara,
lo fuera a disponer,
de quien la noble señora celeste
le había dicho que ya estaba curado.

Y no sólo lo dejaron que fuera,
sino que lo acompañaron allá a su casa.
Y cuando ya llegaron,
vieron a su reverenciado tío
que estaba muy bien,
nada le afligía.
Y él mucho se maravilló
de que su sobrino viniera acompañado
con muchos honores.
Preguntó a su sobrino
por qué ocurría
que tanto lo honraban.

Y él le dijo
que cuando fue allá
a llamar a un sacerdote,
que lo confesara, lo dejara dispuesto,
allá en el Tepeyac
se le apareció la noble señora celeste
y lo envió a México,
a que fuera a ver al gobernante obispo
para que le edificara su casa en el Tepeyac.
Y que ella le dijo que no se afligiera
porque ya estaba él curado,
y con esto mucho se tranquilizó su corazón.

OPPOSITE: The pope in the "pope mobile," on the way to the Basilica of Guadalupe.
OVERLEAF: "John Paul II, the whole world loves you," the people sing at the arrival of the pope
at the Basilica of Guadalupe.

His uncle replied that it was true	su tío le dijo que era verdad,
that she had cured him	que entonces ella lo curó
and that he had seen Her	y que la contempló
in the same manner	de la misma forma
that she had appeared to his nephew.	como se había aparecido a su sobrino.
And he told him	Y le dijo
how she also sent him to Mexico City	cómo también a él lo envió a México
to see the bishop.	para que viera al obispo.
And that also, when he went to see him,	Y también que, cuando fuera a verlo,
that he tell him all he had seen	todo se lo manifestara,
and the wonderful way	le dijera lo que había contemplado
that he had been cured	y el modo maravilloso como lo había curado
and that Her wholly precious image	y que así la llamara,
thus be named	así se nombrara,
Blessed Virgin Mary of Guadalupe.	la del todo doncella
	Santa María de Guadalupe,
	su preciosa imagen.
And they immediately took Juan Bernardino	Y en seguida llevaron a Juan Bernardino
before the governing bishop	delante del que gobierna obispo
so that he may	para que viniera a hablarle,
give testimony before him.	delante de él diera testimonio.
And with his nephew Juan Diego,	Y con su sobrino Juan Diego,
the bishop put them up in his house	los aposentó en su casa el obispo
for a few days	unos pocos días,
while he built the revered house	mientras se levantó la reverenciada casa
of the Noble Heavenly Lady there in Tepeyac	de la noble señora allá en Tepeyac,
where she had shown Juan Diego.	donde se le mostró a Juan Diego.

OPPOSITE: In the Morelos stadium, passion is evident among players who are faithful to the Virgin and pose in front of the tricolor flag for a souvenir photo.
ABOVE: "Bofo" Bautista (left) and Ismael Íñiguez González (right), forwards for the Monarch Team of Morelia, dominate the ball during warm-ups before the game against the Guatemalan national team. They wear the Guadalupan image across their chests.

When the governing bishop	Y cuando el que gobierna obispo
had resided in the great church for some time,	tuvo ya algún tiempo, allá en la iglesia mayor,
he took the precious image	a la preciosa reverenciada imagen
of the Noble Heavenly Lady from where it had been,	de la noble señora celeste,
in the oratory of his palace,	vino a sacarla de su palacio,
so that all the people could	de su oratorio donde estaba,
marvel at Her lovely image.	para que toda la gente viera,
	se maravillara de su preciosa imagen.

And one and all,	Y todos a una,
the entire city was moved	toda la ciudad se conmovió,
when they went to marvel	cuando fue a contemplar,
at the precious image.	fue a maravillarse,
They came to know Her as something divine,	de su preciosa imagen.
and would bring Her requests.	Venían a conocerla como algo divino,
Many were amazed	le hacían súplicas.
at how she had appeared	Mucho se admiraban
by divine nature,	cómo por maravilla divina
seeing that no earthly man	se había aparecido
had painted Her image.	ya que ningún hombre de la tierra
	pintó su preciosa imagen.

ABOVE, LEFT: Some devout octopus fishermen display their catch on the coasts of the state of Guerrero.

ABOVE, RIGHT: A bargeman in Cancún shows his icon with pride.

OPPOSITE: A moving image of a miner who descends the tunnel daily with Guadalupe on his body as well as in his soul.